Digital Coin Creation

Francis Amara

This text will explain and give you an insight on how to create cryptocurrency transactions if you're considering launching your own digital coin and it will give all the necessary approach required for actualization of your set goal for your business irrespective of the size of your establishment.

DIGITAL COIN DEVELOPMENT

BY

FRANCIS AMARA

COPYRIGHT PAGE

Copyright© by Amara Francis 2022. All Right Reserved.

Before this document is duplicated or reproduced in any manner, the publishers consent must be gained. Therefore the contents within can neither be stored electronically, transferred, nor kept in a database. Neither in parts nor full can the document be copied, scanned, faxed, or retained without the approval from the publisher or creator.

TABLE OF CONTENT

Cover page..i

Title page..ii

Copyright..i

Table of content...ii-iii

Dedication..iiii

Preface...v

CHAPTER ONE

1.1. UNDERSTANDING CRYPTOCURRENCY..5
1.2. DEVELOPMENT OF A CRYPTO CURRENCY..6

CHAPTER TWO

2.1 REGIONAL CONSIDERATION IN DIGITAL CURRENCY DEVELOPME.............7

2.2 How To Trade In Cryptocurrencies...7

2.3. Methods For Making Cryptocurrency..8

CHAPTER THREE

3.1 How To Create A Blockchain...8

3.2 Modification Of An Already Existing Blockchain Technology's Code..........8

3.3 A New Cryptocurrency Can Be Created On Existing Blockchain Platform.........9

3.4 The Ethereum Blockchain..10

CHAPTER FOUR

4.1 Making Of A Cryptocurrency...11

4.2. A Step By Step Approach For Developing Your Own Cryptocurreny...............16

CHAPTER FIVE.

5.1 DIGITAL CURRENCIES..17

5.2 Coin vs. Token...17

5.3 What is the price of producing a cryptocurrency..........................18

5.6 Duration for creating a cryptocurrency......................................19

DEDICATION

This informative text is dedicated to all readers globally that always read to seek for knowledge in all ramifications.

Preface

Cryptocurrencies have grown in appeal over the past few years. The earliest and best-known cryptocurrency, Bitcoin, was developed in 2008 and lunched in 2009 with the first successful transaction. Numerous additional cryptocurrencies, including as Ethereum, Litecoin, Ripple and others, have been created since that time.

This text will explain how to create cryptocurrency transactions if you're considering launching your own digital coin.

You might also read more about digital currency and how it can help your business irrespective of the size of your establishment.

Discover more about the sector by reading this rich and informative book for development of cryptocurrency on an already existing blockchain technology and as well as a single blockchain too.

CHAPTER ONE

1. 1. UNDERSTANDING CRYPTOCURRENCY.

This is a decentralized, digital, and virtual currency. Controlled by a peer-to-peer network, and it's transactions frequently take place without any fees or the need for a third party for the success of its transactions.

There are numerous stages to complete before creating a cryptocurrency and promoting it, but the likelihood of being wealthy is significant.

It's not difficult to envision a future in which many of our regular transactions are made across the globe using cryptocurrencies, such as bitcoin, as the market for cryptocurrencies is growing.

Bitcoin for example, Ethereum, PLCU, etc. Consider developing your own blockchain-based currency if you are currently a cryptocurrency developer.

Launch an exchange-traded fund (ETF) for cryptocurrencies to provide your investors the broadest potential portfolio. A cryptocurrency wallet that is integrated with your own crypto-exchange can be made as well.

A tough task that shouldn't be undertaken quickly is starting your own cryptocurrency. It might be worthwhile to look into the possibility of producing your own coin, though, given how many new coins are being released and how unstable the market value is.

Numerous platforms exist that let users mint or mine bitcoin as well as create it and then control the supply. You may create your own platform to gain an advantage over competitors.

Put more of your time and effort into creating a coin that addresses issues in the market. Developed properly, your new money could be the talk of the global coin, like the bitcoin today, before the lunching and legalizing of bitcoin there was no knowledgeable information for its existence, but in the world of crypto today, the statement would not be complete without the mention of Bitcoin particularly.

1.2 DEVELOPMENT OF A CRYPTOCURRENCY

REASON FOR DEVELOPING YOUR COIN.

If you're wondering what cryptocurrency is, proceed. It's crucial to first comprehend what it is.

Cryptography is used by cryptocurrencies to safeguard their transactions and regulate the creation of new units. Cryptocurrencies are digital or virtual tokens. They are also decentralized, which means that neither the government nor financial institutions have any influence over them.

The Securities and Exchange Commission (SECC) has stated that they view Bitcoin and Ethereum as decentralized and secure digital currencies even if they are thought of as such. Additionally, because they are international, cryptocurrencies are a desirable investment for people worldwide. Finally, cryptocurrencies are a wonderful option for those who want to keep their transactions private because they are secure and anonymous.

Thus, we arrive to the progressive business owners might desire to develop their own cryptocurrency because of the cryptnexus of this information here. It turns out there are a number of causes, however the following are the important ones to think about.

CHAPTER TWO

2.1. REGIONAL COSIDERATION IN CRYPTO DEVELOPMENT.

- **Geographical Factors:** When designing a coin or token the below are to be taken into consideration. One might want to design a currency that can be used in a certain nation or area. In this context this is to be considered if the aim of the developer or the owner is looking at creating a token that would be servicing a particular purposes in a particular country, Business portfolio or not.

- **Savings and security:** in this context you can consider designing a currency that is immune to governmental control or inflationary pressures.

- **For loyalty schemes:** You may wish to design a fresh kind of scheme for your patrons. It could be considered to be for a financial support to people or organization or cause.

- **Raise money:** Possessing your own cryptocurrency can be useful when trying to raise money for new ventures or projects.

- **Brand awareness:** Using a cryptocurrency can be a fantastic method to increase brand exposure.

- **It's the future:** Fortune favors the brave, so you'll want to jump the gun and accept this revolutionary technology as soon as possible.

- **To make money:** This article explains how to create a cryptocurrency, however progressive business owners should avoid doing this will eventually want to get into it to generate money following some practice, they'll wish to earn money.

2.2 How To Trade In Cryptocurrencies

Remember that creating your own cryptocurrency market can give you more financial clout if you want to sell products like CBD oil. However, as CBD and companies like it are not a part of the central banking institutions, they are not allowed to participate in the conventional financial sector, not even for routine banking operations.

In the interim, you can create your own cryptocurrency in accordance with the needs of your business and give your CBD business a flexible means of conducting transactions without involving a third party.

2.3. Methods For Making Cryptocurrency

Now that the origin of a cryptocurrency has been clarified,

Let's examine different techniques for producing cryptocurrencies.

CHAPTER THREE

3.1 How To Create A Blockchain

To enable native crypto, you can build your own **blockchain-based-currency** from the ground up. This approach allows you the most design flexibility. However, it takes more than a few clicks to create a new blockchain. The procedure is extremely complicated and calls for at least rudimentary knowledge of coding and a thorough comprehension of blockchain.

In the light of the above, you can hire someone to develop your blockchain if you're not a programmer. Additionally, there are internet tools that make it possible to build a blockchain without any coding knowledge.

3.2 Modification Of An Already Existing Blockchain Technology's Code

This approach or second option to make your own cryptocurrency is to modify an existing blockchain's source code. To generate and introduce a new cryptocurrency, for instance, you can fork the code of an existing coin.

Compared to starting a new blockchain from the scratch, this approach is simpler. It still requires technical knowledge and programming skills, though. Before you make the change to the code, you'll also need to have a solid understanding of how blockchain functions.

Since blockchain requires an infrastructure, it's also a good idea to understand the current blockchain infrastructure of the platform you're working with. If you are completely unfamiliar with this area, you may want to attend a few blockchain classes before diving into its infrastructure needs.

The blockchain architecture you select will rely on the objectives of your project and the resources you have at your disposal. However, you need to have access to the code in order to modify the protocol. Since the majority of blockchains are open source, anyone may access and download them. On the GitHub platform, you may discover the source codes for many of them.

3.3 A New Cryptocurrency Can Be Created On Existing Blockchain Platform

The third cryptocurrency creation method aims to build a new cryptocurrency on a working blockchain. Compared to the previous methods, this one is simpler and doesn't need as much programming experience.

A token, a type of digital money that isn't native to the blockchain will function here, this is what is produced when a new currency is created on the already existing blockchain.

3.4 The Ethereum Blockchain

This emerged as the most popular method for developing new cryptocurrencies on an already-existing blockchain.

An **ERC20 token** is one that is created in this manner.

You must list your ERC20 on cryptocurrency exchanges after you've produced it so that people can buy and trade it. This can be a difficult and expensive operation.

CHAPTER FOUR

4.1 Making Of A Cryptocurrency

Let's address the subject of "How to make a cryptocurrency?" now that we've looked at a few methods for doing so."

As was previously mentioned, Bitcoin was the first decentralized digital currency. It was an enormous success, and the blockchain ecosystem is still expanding. Unfortunately, this does not imply that attempts to create cryptocurrency will be a huge success. In fact, several companies that attempted an ICO failed to secure sufficient money or shut down after their launch.

ICO is an initial coin Offering, it is another form of cryptocurrency that businesses uses to raise capital, through it trading platforms and as well as investors receives a unique currency 'Token' in exchange for their monetary investment in the business.

4.2. A Step By Step Approach For Developing Your Own Cryptocurrency

Here is a step-by-step tutorial on creating a cryptocurrency that can help you successfully establish your own in order to prevent it from happening to you.

a. Specification of your goals.

Consider what you want your coin to do as a first step. Are you in favor of using it as a payment system? Or an investment bank?

Consider the issue that your cryptocurrency will address that other cryptocurrencies do not. You can use this to develop your coin's unique selling proposition (USP). For instance, **Bitcoin was developed as a decentralized substitute for fiat money. On the other hand, Ethereum was created as a platform for programmers to build decentralized applications.**

You must develop a plan when you've determined your goals.

You must come up with a **name and a logo** for your currency after defining your goals. You'll also need to write a **whitepaper and a website**. The website ought to describe your money and how it functions. On the other side, the whitepaper will discuss your idea in greater detail.

Make sure your website and whitepaper are both crystal clear, succinct, and devoid of technical jargon. People won't invest in your project if they can't comprehend what it's aiming to accomplish. That is the key you must have in mind.

b. Create a Mechanism for Consensus

The creation of a consensus mechanism is the next step. This is how **the blockchain state will be agreed**

upon in your coin.

Consensus techniques primarily come in two flavors: proof-of-work **(PoW)** and proof-of-stake **(PoS)**.

The most popular kind of consensus technique is **proof-of-work**. It is the platform used by Bitcoin and the majority of other cryptocurrencies. Miners compete with one another in a PoW system to approve transactions and add blocks to the blockchain. The individual that mines new blocks for is rewarded with crypocurrency.

On the other hand, miners are not required to compete with one another under **proof-of-stake**. To validate transactions, the system instead relies on validators who stake their bitcoin. The value of a validator's vote increases with the amount of cryptocurrency they have staked. PoS has the advantage of being far more energy-efficient than PoW

c. Choose a Blockchain Platform

A blockchain is an immutable ledger for record of transaction that cannot be adjusted, erased or damaged. It is a distributed ledger technology that grant access to a digital information to be recorded and shared but cannot be edited.

You must select your own blockchain platform once you've chosen the consensus method you'll employ.

The Bitcoin blockchain is the obvious solution if a PoW consensus mechanism is what you wish to employ. However, there are a variety of platforms available if you want to adopt PoS, like Ethereum, Cardano, and the quick EOS. Among all the blockchain platform Ethereum is the one of the top choices with a market share of 82.7%

d. Establish The Nodes

After selecting a platform, you'll need to install the software and configure a node.

A node is a computer that keeps a copy of the blockchain, aids in transaction verification, and relays information.

You must sign up for a mining or minting pool if your system is a PoW system. A group of miners who cooperate to mine blocks and split the rewards form a mining pool.

e. Wallet Address Generation

Once your node is configured, you must create a wallet address using the best cryptocurrency wallet choice. When someone wants to purchase your cryptocurrency, they will send money here.

Using an internet service or the computer software, you can create a wallet address.

f. Create The Internal Structure

The internal architecture of your coin must be designed as the following step. This covers elements like the consensus algorithm, network protocol, and transaction format.

You must also choose how many coins you will produce. The supply of your coins is this. Here, it's crucial to create a balance. If you produce an excessive number of coins, their value is probably quite low. However, if you produce too few, customers might not be able to purchase them all.

g. Embedding The APIs

You must integrate the APIs after creating the internal architecture of your cryptocurrency. Different software applications can connect with one another thanks to the API (Application Programming Interface).

For instance, integrating the Bitcoin API will enable your cryptocurrency to communicate with the Bitcoin blockchain if you intend to utilize a proof-of-work (PoW) mechanism. You must incorporate the Ethereum API in order for your coin to communicate with the Ethereum blockchain if you wish to use a PoS scheme. Here is a list of the best blockchain APIs.

Top Blockchain API Platforms.

The underlisted are the Blockchain Platforms to be considered as the case may be.

Ethereum market leader of 82.70% share capital.

Waves

Hyper ledger fabrics

NEM

IBM Blockchain

Blockstarter

Bigchain DB

EOS

Ripple

Quorum

IOTA

CoinList

Multichain

Openchain

Chaincore.

If you have the future plan for a successful and a progressive business interest, put setting up the foundation of your own cryptocurrency in the present into considerations.

You're almost ready to launch your coin once you've integrated the APIs.

h. Legalize Your Cryptocurrency

Making your cryptocurrency legal is the last step, and there are set guidelines for allowing the production of coins. Creating a business and obtaining a license from the government are required for this.

Your cryptocurrency must also be registered with the Financial Crimes Enforcement Network (FinCEN). This is the US government organization in charge of preventing the financing of terrorism and money laundering.

Finally, have in mind that some nations forbid the use of cryptocurrencies, so before it launches, you should check the regulations in your country.

Once you've completed everything, kudos! You're ready to launch your coin!

i. Get Your New Cryptocurrency Growing

Even if there are many technical considerations when creating a cryptocurrency, it's crucial to concentrate on marketing and promotion of your new coin.

Your cryptocurrency is likely to fail without acceptance. Therefore, be sure to invest some effort in promoting the use and acceptance of your currency. Giving away your coin for free is a smart approach to advertise it. You can achieve this by distributing a specific number of brand-new cryptocurrency coins to early adopters or by launching marketing efforts.

Additionally, you ought to think about putting your coin on exchanges. This will make it easy for others to buy and trade your currency. Finally, you should be ready to respond to inquiries concerning your cryptocurrency. Make sure you have the answers they're seeking for because there will likely be many questions.

CHAPTER FIVE.

5.1 DIGITAL CURRENCIES.

Coin and Token are known as digital currencies and serves same purpose of transactions in different aspect.

In this context you will understand that coins are globally used and generally accepted while Token are limited to a Geographical region or area, thereby limiting its use.

5.2 Coin vs. Token

COIN

a. Coin is a part of a single blockchain.

b. Coin is universal.

c. Coin can buy Token

d. Coin is globally accepted

TOKEN.

    a. This operates on an already existing blockchain.
    b. Limited to a specific industries or regional zone.
    c. Token cannot buy coin.

Cryptocurrencies come in the form of either coins or tokens. It can be difficult to make your own coin or token. Although both are digital assets, there are important distinctions between the two.

Cryptocurrencies stand alone as separate currencies. For instance, Bitcoin is a cryptocurrency coin that doesn't require the existence of another platform. Another well-known cryptocurrency coin with a corresponding digital asset that denotes some kind of utility or value is Ethereum.

A cryptocurrency coin is a form of decentralized digital money that controls the generation of new units of the currency and utilizes encryption to safeguard its transactions.

Cryptocurrency coins include Bitcoin, Ether, Ripple, and Litecoin, etc.

A cryptocurrency token, which is also a smart contract, is a digital asset that is created to use on a specific platform. On a blockchain-based platform, crypto tokens are frequently used to represent an asset or utility. For instance, the Golem Network Token (GNT), a decentralized supercomputer that anybody may utilize, is used there. GNT is a utility token in this instance that enables users to access and utilize the Golem network.

Ether, the native cryptocurrency of the Ethereum blockchain, was mentioned earlier. It is a cryptocurrency token as well. It typically goes by the name "ERC20 token" since it adheres to a particular set of guidelines on the blockchain of Ethereum (ERC stands for Ethereum Request for Comment). These tokens can be used to represent anything, including a physical object as well as digital assets and services.

Also, If you want to establish your own solo money, then you'll need to develop a cryptocurrency coin. However, if you want to use blockchain technology to create a new application or service, then you'll need to create your own token.

So, to summarize, A cryptocurrency coin has its own currency and doesn't require another platform to operate. A couple of instances of cryptocurrency coins include bitcoin and ether.

A cryptocurrency coin token is a digital asset that's designed to utilize on a certain platform. Cryptocurrency tokens include ether and the Golem Network Token (GNT).

5.3 What Is The Price Of Producing a Cryptocurrency.

Depending on your business and the type of cryptocurrency you wish to manufacture, the price will change requirements. The cost will be relatively low if you just want to make a basic cryptocurrency coin. The price will be higher if you want to develop a more complicated application or service, though.

According to Develop Coins, the cost of developing a cryptocurrency ranges from $10,000 to $30,000. On the other hand, Devteam.space states that the range is lower. The cost to create the software, write and launch a whitepaper is somewhere around $6,000 to $10,000.

5.6 Duration for creating a cryptocurrency.

Depending on how hard it is, it might take you anywhere from one to six months to create a new coin from start. Depending on your level of technical understanding, modifying the existing encryption code will take a different amount of time. The process may take four hours if you are skilled. You may make a new currency in as little as 5 to 20 minutes if you employ automated tools.

You now have access to a detailed manual on how to create a Cryptocurrency.

We hope you found this article to be useful and educational and that the business idea of creating your own digital currency intrigued you. The future If you follow these suggestions.

www.ingramcontent.com/pod-product-compliance
Lightning Source LLC
Chambersburg PA
CBHW050328220526
45465CB00005B/2182